100 FACTS
Spiders

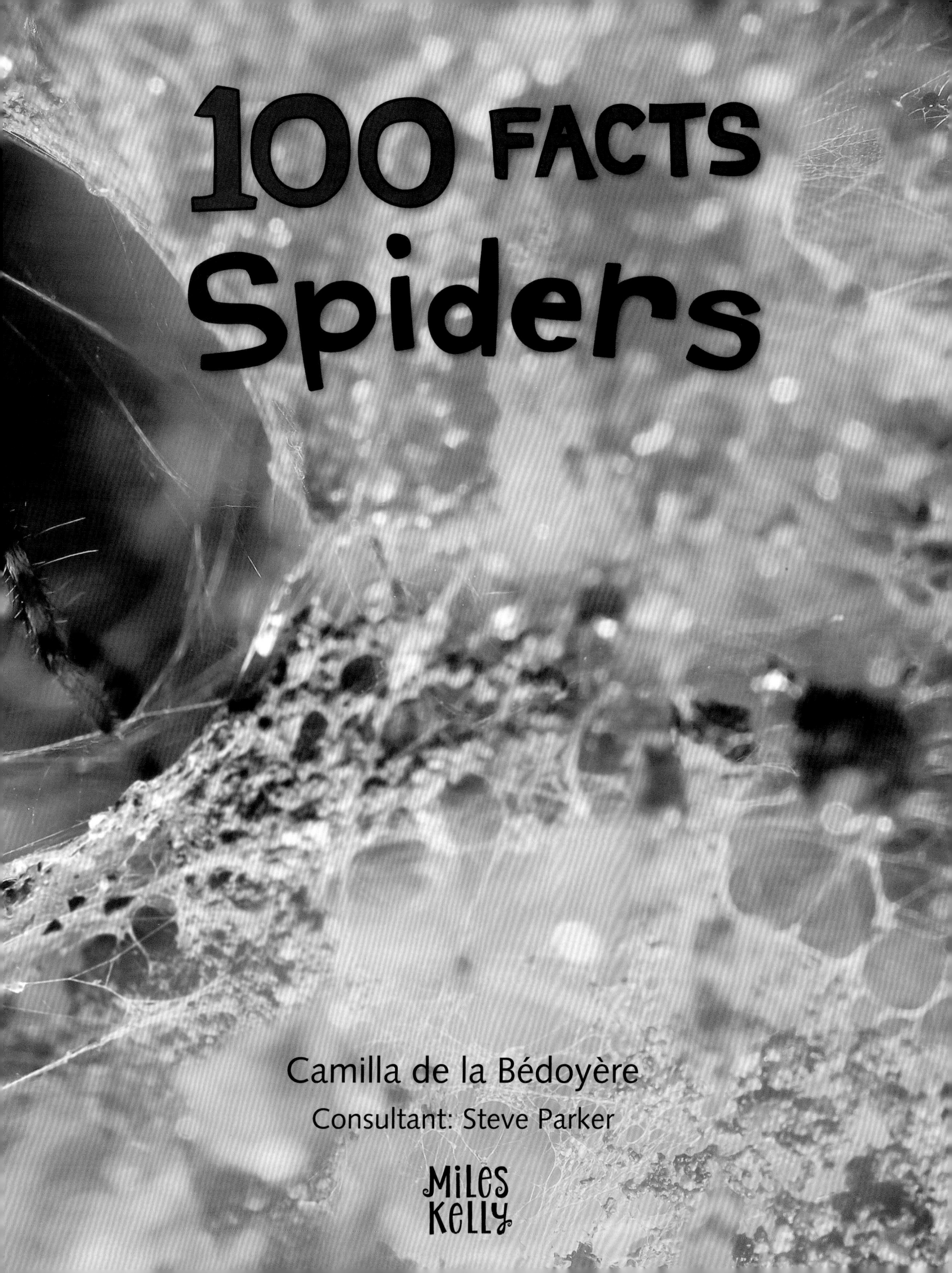

100 FACTS
Spiders

Camilla de la Bédoyère

Consultant: Steve Parker

Miles Kelly

First published in 2011 by Miles Kelly Publishing Ltd
Harding's Barn, Bardfield End Green, Thaxted, Essex, CM6 3PX, UK

Copyright © Miles Kelly Publishing Ltd 2011

10 12 14 15 13 11

Publishing Director Belinda Gallagher
Creative Director Jo Cowan
Editorial Director Rosie Neave
Senior Editors Sarah Carpenter, Becky Miles
Editorial Assistant Lauren White
Managing Designer Simon Lee
Volume Designer Andrea Slane
Image Manager Liberty Newton
Indexer Eleanor Holme
Production Controller Elizabeth Collins
Reprographics Stephan Davis
Assets Venita Kidwai

All rights reserved. No part of this publication may be reproduced, stored in a retrieval system, or transmitted by any means, electronic, mechanical, photocopying, recording or otherwise, without the prior permission of the copyright holder.

ISBN 978-1-78989-391-5

Printed in China
British Library Cataloguing-in-Publication Data
A catalogue record for this book is available from the British Library

ACKNOWLEDGEMENTS

The publishers would like to thank the following artists who have contributed to this book:
Julian Baker, Mike Foster (Maltings Partnership), Ian Jackson, Mike Saunders
Cover artwork: Ian Jackson

All other artworks are from the Miles Kelly Artwork Bank

The publishers would like to thank the following sources for the use of their photographs:
t = top, b = bottom, l = left, r = right, c = centre

Cover (back) Tomatito/ShutterstockPremier
Alamy 20(bg) Susan & Allan Parker; 23(tr) Morley Read/Alamy; 37(tr) Brian Hewitt; 44(bl) Imagebroker.net; 45(b) Columbia Pictures, Marvel Enterprises **Ardea** 21(tr) Brian Bevan; 37(bl) Steve Hopkin **Diomedia** 39(tr) Science Source/Larry West **Dreamstime** 20(tr) & 24(tc) Cathykeifer; 44(t) Thierry Maffeis **FLPA** 13(b) Piotr Naskrecki/Minden Pictures; 14(bl), 18(bl) & 43(cr) & (br) Mark Moffett/Minden Pictures; 15 Michael & Patricia Fogden/Minden Pictures; 22(bl) Larry West; 25(br) Thomas Marent/Minden Pictures; 26(cr) Richard Becker; 27(tr) Heidi & Hans-Juergen Koch/Minden Pictures **Fotolia** 12(paper, c) deardone; 28(l) Cathy Keifer **iStockphoto.com** 6–7 Atelopus; 41 ElementalImaging **Moviestore Collection** 45(t) Paramount Pictures, Walden Media, K Entertainment Company, Nickelodeon Movies, KMP Film Invest, Sandman Studios **NaturePL** 17(b), 22(t), 35(tr) & 47(tr) Stephen Dalton; 18–19 Simon Colmer; 26(l) Ingo Arndt; 27(b) Nick Upton; 30(b) Solvin Zankl; 35 Stephen Dalton; 40–41(bg) Kim Taylor **Photoshot** 31(b) Stephen Dalton; 42(bl) Jany Sauvanet **ShutterstockPremier** 2–3 zroakez; 9(tl) & (tr) BHJ; 12(br) Tobik; 17(t) ctpaul; 33(br) Lidara; 34–35(bg) Dean Pennala

All other photographs are from:digitalvision, Corel, PhotoDisc

Every effort has been made to acknowledge the source and copyright holder of each picture.
Miles Kelly Publishing apologises for any unintentional errors or omissions.

Made with paper from a sustainable forest

www.mileskelly.net

Contents

Fanged and ferocious 6

What is a spider? 8

Shapes and sizes 10

Fearsome family 12

Super spider senses 14

Smooth movers 16

Spider mates 18

Spiderlings 20

Where spiders live 22

Super silk 24

Weaving and building 26

On the menu 28

On the run 30

Death by stealth 32

Orb-web spiders 34

Funnel web spiders 36

Widows and wolves 38

Jumping spiders 40

Tarantulas 42

Spiders and us 44

SOS – save our spiders 46

Index 48

Fanged and ferocious

1 **Spiders may be small, but they are fast-moving, ferocious hunters.** These eight-legged mini-beasts inspire fear in many people, but most of them are harmless to humans. Spiders are important predators of flies and other pests. They are also food for other animals, especially birds and insects.

▶ Zoom in close to a tropical wolf spider feeding on a centipede! Spiders are not just creepy-crawlies — they are fascinating creatures with an incredible way of life.

What is a spider?

2 Spiders belong to a group of animals called arachnids. They have eight legs unlike insects, which have six. Almost all spiders live on land and are predators – they hunt other animals to eat.

TRUE OR FALSE?
1. Spiders are insects.
2. Predators are animals that eat grass.
3. A spider's palps inject venom into prey.

Answers:
All are false

3 A spider's body is divided into two parts, which are connected by a slender stalk. The front part of the body is called a cephalothorax (say: kef-a-low-thor-ax) and the rear part is called the abdomen.

▼ Like many animals, spiders have organs inside their bodies. The organs carry out essential jobs, such as digesting food and circulating blood.

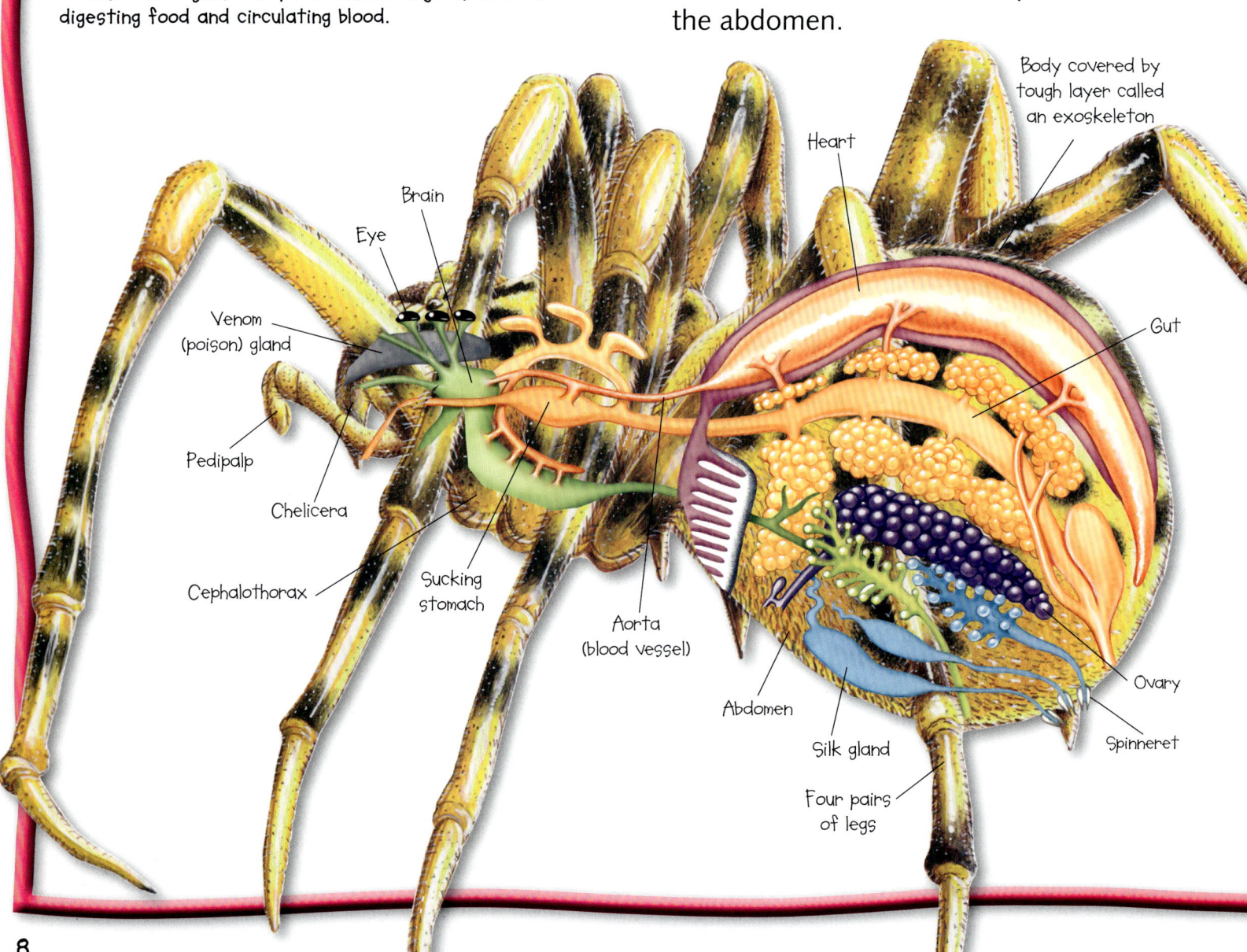

Brain · Eye · Venom (poison) gland · Pedipalp · Chelicera · Cephalothorax · Sucking stomach · Aorta (blood vessel) · Abdomen · Silk gland · Four pairs of legs · Heart · Body covered by tough layer called an exoskeleton · Gut · Ovary · Spinneret

▲ Garden spiders have large, swollen abdomens. The small, black eyes are visible at the front of the head.

▲ These common arachnids have three pairs of spinnerets at the tips of their abdomens.

4 **Spiders can make threads of super-strong silk.** They can build with it, throw it and wind it. Because spiders can make silk, they have been able to survive in most land habitats. One type of spider even uses its silk to live underwater.

5 **Pedipalps, chelicerae and spinnerets are useful tools for spiders.** Leg-like pedipalps are short feelers, fangs in the chelicerae inject deadly venom (poison) into prey, and spinnerets produce silk to wrap prey up.

6 **About 40,000 species (types) of spiders have been named so far.** There are plenty more waiting to be discovered. These animals walked our planet long before the dinosaurs and have been around for at least 300 million years.

Shapes and sizes

7 Almost every spider in the world is smaller than your hand. Most of them are even smaller than your little finger. However, there are some giants and midgets in the arachnid family – and some spiders that don't even look like spiders!

MAKING SPIDERS
You will need:
scissors   egg carton
pipe cleaners   coloured pens

Cut out each section of an egg carton. Each one will be a spider's body. Poke pipe cleaners through the sides to make the legs. Decorate the body with eyes and markings.

8 Goliath bird-eating spiders are enormous, but they don't normally eat birds. Goliaths eat mostly bugs, mice, lizards and frogs. The world's largest spider is the giant huntsman spider. It has a leg span of 30 centimetres, and lives in caves in Laos, in Southeast Asia.

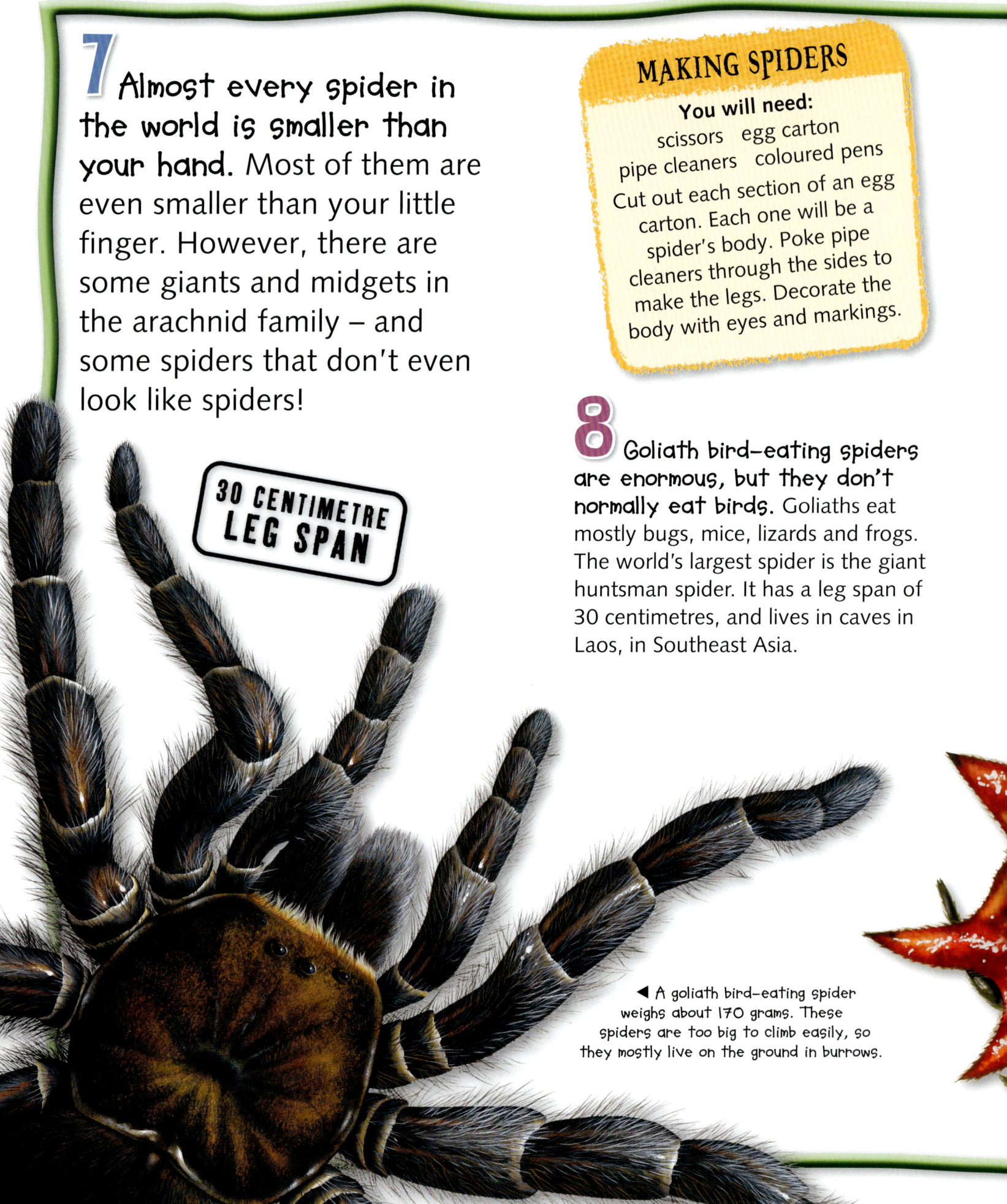

30 CENTIMETRE LEG SPAN

◀ A goliath bird-eating spider weighs about 170 grams. These spiders are too big to climb easily, so they mostly live on the ground in burrows.

9 **Crab spiders look and move just like crabs.** The females have large, round bodies, and they can scuttle backwards or sideways when scared. Some crab spiders have pointed humps on their abdomens and little horns on their heads.

▲ Female spiders are often bigger than males. This is especially true of crab spiders. The females are often more colourful too.

10 **Not all spiders have a round body and long legs.** Ant spiders look just like weaver ants, and peacock spiders have beautiful colours more often seen in birds. The bird dung spider has the best disguise – it looks like bird poo!

▼ A male peacock spider raises its body and legs to show off its beautiful colours.

◄ Spiny orb weavers are often boldly coloured, and have spines or horns on their bodies.

11 **Midget spiders are the smallest spiders in the world.** Their bodies are usually no more than 5 millimetres long. One male found on the island of Western Samoa measured just 0.43 millimetres – smaller than a pinhead. Their webs can be less than 10 millimetres across.

Fearsome family

12 Spiders have some fearsome relatives. Scorpions, ticks and mites all belong to the arachnid family. Other less fearsome family members are false scorpions, harvestmen and sun-spiders.

13 Scorpions are the oldest of all arachnids. Fossils show that some scorpions have reached lengths of nearly 90 centimetres. Larger species are usually less venomous than smaller ones. The most dangerous species is the death-stalker scorpion.

▲ Scorpions have large pincers and nasty stings in their tails.

▶ There are different types or 'orders' of animals in the Arachnid class.

CLASS: *Arachnida*

- ORDER: *Areneida* Spiders
- ORDER: *Scorpiones* Scorpions
- ORDER: *Parasitiformes* Ticks and mites
- ORDER: *Opilones* Harvestmen
- ORDER: *Solpugida* Sun-spiders

14 Ticks and mites are tiny arachnids that can survive in almost every land habitat. Miniature mites are not even one millimetre long, and most live and feed on other animals and plants. Many types of ticks are pests that suck the blood of animals and humans, spreading disease.

▼ When ticks start to drink blood, their soft bodies stretch as they swell, so there is space for more.

◀ Tiny red velvet mites are often found in gardens. They live in soil and feed on insects.

I DON'T BELIEVE IT!
Scientists are hoping to use scorpion venom to cure all kinds of medical problems. Chinese doctors have known for centuries that venom can be used as a powerful painkiller.

▲ Harvestmen are often mistaken for spiders. However, these arachnids have just one rounded body part and not two, like spiders.

15 **Sun-spiders have enormous biting chelicerae.** However, they don't have venom. They use sucker pads on their pedipalps to hold their prey down, while chewing with their pincer-like chelicerae. Sun-spiders feed on insects and pests, such as termites.

16 **Harvestmen have small bodies and eight long, skinny legs.** They have a cunning trick for survival – if attacked, they shed one of their legs, which continues to move! The predator is distracted by the twitching leg while the harvestman makes a quick getaway on its remaining legs!

▶ Sun-spiders have ten or 11 segments in their abdomens. The abdomen of a spider has no segments.

Segment

Super spider senses

Jumping spider

Crab spider

Ogre-faced spider

Spitting spider

▲ Spiders with large eyes need to see in the dark or focus on prey.

▼ A male tarantula strokes strands of silk at the entrance to a female's burrow. She senses the movement and comes out.

17 Although spiders have several eyes, they don't rely on their eyesight. Taste, smell and vibration are all important in helping spiders find their way around, locate prey and avoid being eaten!

18 Most spiders have eight eyes, which are arranged in two or three rows at the front of the head. Their main eyes can see images in focus and with detail, while their side eyes spot movement. It is thought that all spiders may be able to see in colour. However, like insects, spiders probably can't see the colour red.

19 **Spiders are very hairy!** This helps them to hunt, because the tiny hairs are very sensitive to being moved by air and touch. Spiders also have tiny areas, called slit organs, dotted around their exoskeletons. Cave spiders are completely blind, but they can find a fly 30 centimetres away by using the information they get from their hairs and slit organs.

▶ The legs of a Mexican red-knee tarantula are covered with touch-sensitive hairs.

◀ Jumping spiders use the four large eyes on the front of their heads to see their prey and judge distance when hunting.

TOUCHY-FEELY TEATIME
Ask a grown up to prepare a meal that you can eat using your fingers. Cover your eyes with a blindfold and try to identify the foods using your senses of touch, smell and taste.

20 **Spiders don't have tongues and noses — they use their legs to taste and smell!** A spider may have as many as 1000 special hairs on each leg that can detect smell and taste. A quick prod will tell a spider if a dead fly is fresh and can be eaten, or old and rotting and should be left alone.

▶ Ogre-faced, or net-casting, spiders have big eyes so they can see at night. They focus on their prey as they throw a silken net over it.

21 **Spiders that use their eyes to find prey are often active in the day.** They usually hunt and grab their prey. Spiders that rely more on their touch senses are nocturnal, which means they are most active at night. Nocturnal spiders usually catch their prey in silken webs or traps.

Smooth movers

22 Spiders can run very fast. The fastest spider ever recorded was a female house spider, covering a distance 330 times her own body length in ten seconds! Spiders can't keep running for long before they become exhausted.

I DON'T BELIEVE IT!
If a sprinter wanted to run as fast as the world's fastest house spider, he would need to hit speeds of 216 kilometres an hour!

▼ Wolf spiders are all-round athletes! They can walk, stalk, run and even skate on water when they pursue their prey.

23 Moving eight legs takes a lot of energy and co-ordination, so spiders usually move just four legs at a time. When a spider walks it might use the first and third leg on its left side, and the second and fourth leg on its right side, while the other four legs rest. The rested legs then take the next step.

24 Young spiders have little legs, so they take to the skies to move long distances. They face the wind and throw a silken thread into the air. The wind lifts them up and carries them away – this is called 'ballooning'. Pilots have seen ballooning spiders at heights of several thousand metres!

◀ The underside of a spider's foot is covered in hairs. Each hair is split into microscopic end-feet.

Tufts of hair, called scopulae
Claw

▲ Claws on the end of a spider's feet help it to grasp silk threads and walk along them.

25 **Spiders can walk on smooth surfaces.** Their feet, which are called tarsi, are covered with thick tufts of hair. Each hair is divided into thousands of tiny parts, called end-feet. The end-feet stick to walls so well that a spider can raise several feet at once without falling off.

▼ Being able to walk on water has given this raft spider an advantage over land spiders. It has been able to grab a large, juicy stickleback fish to eat.

26 **Lots of spiders are able to walk on water.** Raft spiders use this skill to find food. They rest their front legs on the water's surface to sense vibrations caused by animals beneath. When a fish or tadpole comes close, the raft spider glides over the water and grabs it.

Spider mates

27 When male spiders are old enough to mate, they often stop eating. They put all their energy into finding a female. Many males die soon after mating.

28 Male spiders perform courtship dances to impress the females. Every species has its own courtship routine, so females can recognize males of their species. Male scaffold web spiders rub part of their carapace (shell-like covering over the cephalothorax) against their abdomen, making a loud noise to call females.

▼ A male garden spider attaches a special mating thread to the female's web. He taps the thread, and the female comes to investigate.

Female

◄ Male jumping spiders raise their legs in a mating display called a courtship.

29 **Male ornate jumping spiders have clever tricks to attract females.** They position themselves on leaves in full sunlight and begin to dance. Their bodies have special scales that reflect ultraviolet light. The females' eyes detect it as a glow. They walk towards the glow, and the males drum the leaves with their feet, to keep the females' attention.

Male

I DON'T BELIEVE IT!
Female spiders are usually bigger than males. If a male tries to mate with a female who isn't interested in him, or who has already mated, she may treat him like prey and swiftly bite and eat him.

30 **When two male wolf spiders want to mate with the same female they will fight.** They lift their legs to threaten one another, and the smaller male usually scuttles away. Males sometimes grasp one another with their strong chelicerae.

31 **It is often said that female spiders eat their mates.** However, most males escape unharmed. Some smart male crab spiders wrap the females up in silk before mating, then run away before they break free. Others present their mates with packages of food.

Spiderlings

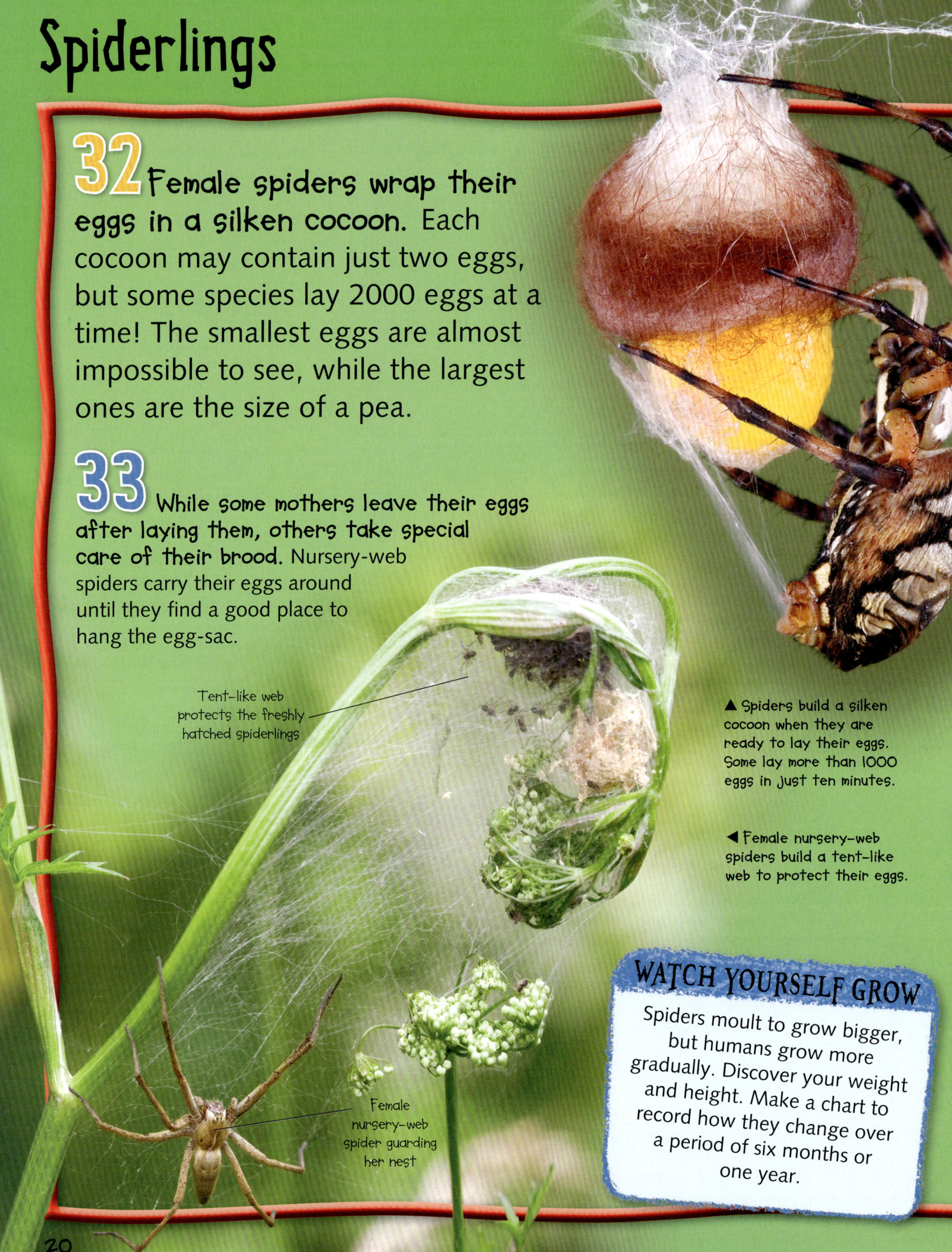

32 Female spiders wrap their eggs in a silken cocoon. Each cocoon may contain just two eggs, but some species lay 2000 eggs at a time! The smallest eggs are almost impossible to see, while the largest ones are the size of a pea.

33 While some mothers leave their eggs after laying them, others take special care of their brood. Nursery-web spiders carry their eggs around until they find a good place to hang the egg-sac.

Tent-like web protects the freshly hatched spiderlings

▲ Spiders build a silken cocoon when they are ready to lay their eggs. Some lay more than 1000 eggs in just ten minutes.

◄ Female nursery-web spiders build a tent-like web to protect their eggs.

Female nursery-web spider guarding her nest

WATCH YOURSELF GROW
Spiders moult to grow bigger, but humans grow more gradually. Discover your weight and height. Make a chart to record how they change over a period of six months or one year.

34 Baby spiders are called spiderlings. Wolf spider mothers use their mouthparts to open their chelicerae, so the spiderlings can get out. Up to 100 spiderlings quickly climb onto their mother's abdomen and hold on to its hairy surface.

▲ A wolf spider carrying its young on its back. The spiderlings stay there for about a week, before they clamber down and head off for independent lives.

35 Some mothers provide food for their spiderlings. Female cobweb spiders produce droplets of liquid that emerge from their mouths. Spiderlings suck up the liquid, which comes from the mother's stomach and is made up of food that is partly digested.

▼ Small males may only need to moult twice before they reach adulthood, but large females may have to moult up to ten times.

① The spider hangs upside down from a moulting thread.

② The old exoskeleton splits and cracks open.

③ The spider pulls its legs and abdomen free.

  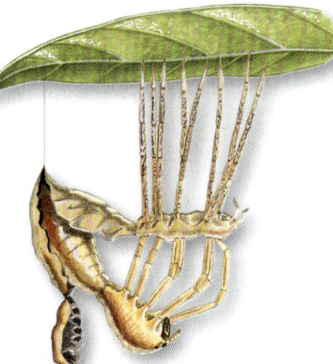

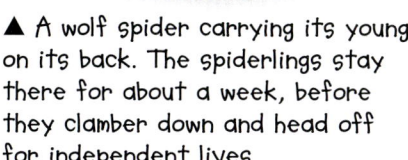

④ The new exoskeleton is soft and bendy. The spider quickly bends all of its leg joints while its skin dries.

36 Baby spiders look just like their parents, but are much smaller. As they grow, spiders moult (shed) their tough outer skin (exoskeleton). The old skin comes away and the spider grows bigger as a new one forms.

Where spiders live

▲ Adult cave spiders hide from light. When their spiderlings hatch from a cocoon, they find new homes by running towards light.

37 There are spiders in the Arctic, in deserts, by the sea and even on top of mountains. They are most common in places where there are lots of plants. Spiders live under stones and plants, and in fields, farms, forests and buildings.

▼ Beach wolf spiders blend in with their sandy homes. Patterns on their skin help them to hide from predators.

38 Spiders living in cool places find it hard to survive the winter. The cold and shortage of food means that few of these species are active during the coldest times of year. Some of them dig into leaf litter and rest, or hibernate, until spring. Others lay their eggs before winter and die, and the eggs then hatch in spring.

I DON'T BELIEVE IT!
Young water spiders can't spin themselves a silken home, so they take over empty pond snail shells and fill them with air to breathe.

39 **Most spiders live alone, but there are a few friendly types.** Lynx spiders live in warm tropical rainforests and work together to build large webs. The groups, or colonies, contain hundreds of spiders, including males, females and spiderlings.

40 **There is only one type of spider in the world that can live in water.** It can be difficult for air-breathing animals to live underwater. The water spider traps bubbles of air from the surface and takes them to its underwater web. It mates, lays eggs and eats its prey inside the waterproof silken structure.

▲ Spiders that live and work together are called social spiders. This way of life is rare for arachnids.

41 **In 1924 an explorer found spiders living at a height of 6700 metres on Mount Everest.** The spiders were sheltering from the extreme weather by hiding under stones. It is thought these spiders survive by eating food carried up the mountain by the wind.

▶ A water spider carries a bubble of air underwater. It will use the bubble to top up the air supplies inside its silken home, which is called a retreat.

Super silk

◀ A grasshopper is caught inside a web of super-strong silk. The spider keeps wrapping the silk around the insect's body to make a neat little package.

42 **All spiders are able to make silk.** The silken threads are made of protein and produced in special silk glands. Its unique qualities make it one of the most incredible substances on Earth.

43 **Scientists would love to unravel silk's many secrets.** No fibres made by humans can match silk's strength and elasticity (stretchiness). It can stretch up to six times its length before snapping. Silk could be used to make ultra-tough fabric for sportspeople or people who work in dangerous places. If a 20-millimetre-thick fibre of silk could be made, it could lift a truck.

QUIZ

1. What are a spider's silken threads made of?
2. Where are they produced?
3. What do weaver ants use their larvae's silk for?

Answers:
1. Protein 2. In special silk glands 3. To build huge nests

Larva
Adult ant
Silk

44 **Spiders can make different kinds of silk.** Some threads are dry but extremely strong, while other kinds are moist and elastic. Spiders use different silk for different jobs, such as making webs or cocoons to protect their eggs.

▲ Green tree ants are a type of weaver ant. They use their larvae's silk to build huge nests.

▼ Butterfly and moth larvae also make silk. Spindle ermine moth larvae have covered this tree with silken webs.

45 **Spiders are not the only animals that can make silk.** Adult weaver ants use their larvae as silk-making machines! These insects use leaves to make nests at the tops of trees. When they need to bind the leaves together, the ants grab their larvae and move them from side to side. The silk that the larvae produce hold the leaf edges together.

46 **Spider silk is coated in a sticky 'glue'.** Scientists have been trying to find a way to copy this 'glue', because it is very strong. It could possibly be made from cheaper, more environmentally friendly ingredients than other glues (which are often made from oil).

Weaving and building

47 Spiders use their strong silken threads for many things. Silk is used to make draglines to travel, to protect eggs, to hide from predators and to wrap up prey. Many spiders also use silk to build traps and webs.

48 Silk glands inside the abdomen produce liquid silk. It is up to 300,000 times lighter than solid silk. Each gland leads to a spinneret, with an opening called a spigot. When the liquid silk is forced towards the spigot, its tiny particles line up into long fibres and turn solid. The spider's abdomen and spinnerets help the spider direct its threads.

◀ Silken threads are incredibly fine, but they are strong enough to support the weight of a spider.

▲ Silk emerges from an orbweaver's spigot. The spider uses its feet to pull the threads out.

WONDERFUL WEBS

Find several spiders' webs. Use a sketchbook and pencil to copy the patterns and shapes of the webs. Can you see the spiders that built each one?

49 Some spiders build beautiful, tidy webs that are stretched out like nets. Others make scruffy, disorganized meshes of silk. Daddy longlegs spiders make some of the untidiest webs of all.

▲ Daddy longlegs spiderlings stay in their mother's messy web when they hatch.

50 Spiders that build sheet webs weave flat, silken mats and hide underneath them. Silken threads hang down onto the sheets, and when the spider senses an insect's movement, it shakes its web. The insect falls into the sheet and the spider tears through the web to bite its prey.

51 Spiders recycle their silk. When traps and webs get old they lose their strength and stretchiness. Spiders eat the threads and the silk proteins are reused to make more silk in their silk glands.

▼ A female money spider hangs upside-down below her delicate sheet web. When finished, the sheet will be a dome shape, constructed from ultra-fine threads of silk.

On the menu

52 Almost all spiders are carnivores — they eat other animals. They prey on insects or other invertebrates (animals without backbones), especially spiders.

◀ A female green lynx spider has its fangs in a fly. All spiders are equipped with venom, which is a deadly poison that paralyzes victims (stops them from moving). It is injected by fangs on their chelicerae.

53 Crab spiders prey on large insects, such as butterflies. They don't eat the tough exoskeleton, so the butterfly's remains look almost untouched after the spider has finished its meal.

▲ A gold leaf crab spider bites a hole in a honeybee's body. It then sucks out the insect's insides.

54 Orbweaving spiders trap their prey, bite it, wrap it in silk and wait for it to die. They vomit digestive juices over their prey, turning it to liquid. Then the spiders suck the liquid up. The mouthparts of most spiders are lined with tiny hairs, which act like a filter when sucking up liquid.

55 Only one type of spider is known to be mostly vegetarian. *Bagheera kiplingi* spiders feast on tasty nodules that grow on acacia trees. They sometimes also suck nectar from flowers. However, they do occasionally feed on ant larvae.

QUIZ

1. Is a meat eater called a carnivore or a carnival?
2. Is the tough outer skin of an insect or spider called leather or exoskeleton?
3. If something is nutritious, is it a good food or a poisonous newt?

Answers:
1. A carnivore 2. Exoskeleton 3. A good food

On the run

56 For millions of years, spiders have been in a battle for survival. Their success is largely thanks to the incredible ways they defeat, or avoid, predators. The main danger comes from other spiders, but they have tricks to outsmart all attackers.

57 Spiders can run fast or 'fly' to make a quick getaway. They don't have wings, but spiders can throw a lasso of silk, called a dragline, to a nearby plant or twig and swing out of harm's way.

▲ Funnel web spiders look scary when they rear up. They can move fast but they can't jump.

58 Some spiders are masters of arachnobatics! Somersaulting spiders of the Sahara desert can whizz down a sand dune by doing flips and cartwheels. However, spiders can overdo the gymnastics – too many flips and turns can exhaust a spider so much that it dies.

◄ A golden wheel spider rolls down a sand dune to escape a predator. It can reach a top speed of 2 metres per second – that's as fast as a person cartwheeling the length of a football pitch in two seconds!

▶ Ant-mimic spiders look and walk like ants! This clever trick scares off some predators, and allows the spiders to sneak into other spiders' nests to feed on their eggs.

59 **Male funnel web spiders don't run away — they stand their ground.** When it is time to mate, the males come out of their burrows to look for females. If they meet humans, they may rear up and lunge forward to bite. Some types of funnel web have deadly venom, but others are harmless to humans.

I DON'T BELIEVE IT!
If a young spider loses a leg or two after being attacked, it can grow new ones! The legs look normal, but they don't have quite the same muscle power as the original legs had.

60 **Smart spiders play dead when they are attacked.** They fall to the ground and pull their legs up. Dead, dry spiders do not look as appetising as fresh, living ones, so predators leave them alone. The spider leaps up and runs off once the predator has gone away.

▶ Playing dead can be risky. Some animals don't mind eating dead spiders!

Death by stealth

61 Spiders can be divided into two groups — those that hunt their prey and those that catch or trap it. The spiders that hunt their prey are often called 'wandering spiders' and have special skills.

62 Spiders that hunt at night are often dark in colour and covered in lots of fine hairs. Their colour helps them to stay hidden and the hairs, along with their sensory slit organs, help them to detect vibrations caused by other creatures' movement.

◀ Spitting spiders spit a mixture of venom and 'glue' at their prey. They can attack from a distance of 10 millimetres away — nearly twice their body length.

63 Spitting spiders blast a jet of sticky poison at their prey. The lethal liquids are fired at lightning speed, giving the victim no time to escape. The spider can then bite its prey to death and devour its meal.

64 The mouse spider creeps around houses, stealthily stalking prey. During the day these hunters rest in a silken home, hidden from view. At night they search for flies, moths and mosquitoes and leap on them, delivering a deadly bite.

The trapdoor is disguised with plants and soil

◀ When an unsuspecting bug walks over the trapdoor, the spider leaps out to catch it.

Some burrows have side chambers, where the spider lurks

The spider may hide under a flap at the bottom of the hole

65 **Trapdoor spiders lurk in burrows that are hidden from view.** They build a trapdoor that covers the entrance to the burrow, and cover it with plants and soil. The trapdoor is made of silk and the tunnels are lined with silk.

I DON'T BELIEVE IT!
Brazilian wandering spiders have the largest venom glands of all spiders. They have enough venom to kill 225 mice.

▼ A crab spider's front two pairs of legs are longer and stronger than its other legs. It uses them to reach forward and grab prey.

66 **Spiders are perfectly suited to their habitats.** Female crab spiders are often coloured to match the flowers they live on, and some types can even change colour. Wandering insects walk right past the spiders, which are almost invisible.

Orb-web spiders

67 Orb-web spiders create the most extraordinary silk structures. They use the least amount of silk necessary to build the largest traps. One spider can weave an entire web in just 30 minutes.

68 When we think of spiders' webs, we usually think of an orb web. However, fewer than 10 percent of spiders build webs like these. Most orb webs are built in the evening or early hours of the morning. They are almost invisible unless dew or rain settles on the strands.

▶ The hardest part of building a web is getting the first thread in place. The spider needs a gust of wind to carry the thread across, so it sticks to a good spot.

① The first thread is horizontal

② The second thread makes a Y-shape

③ More strands, called radials, are added

④ A temporary spiral is put in place

⑤ The final spiral is built more carefully

▶ Tiny cucumber spiders can build orb webs between two sides of a leaf.

▲ Early morning dew often destroys webs. Garden spiders have to repair or rebuild their webs almost every day.

70 The smallest orb webs are built by midget spiders. These are the smallest spiders in the world. One of their webs may be less than 10 millimetres from one side to the other.

I DON'T BELIEVE IT!
Spiders don't learn how to build webs — they just know how to do it. In fact, young spiders usually build better, neater webs than older spiders!

69 Orb weaver spiders build their webs near water, because flying insects often live nearby. Their brown, velvety bodies are camouflaged against the fences, bridges and buildings where they often set their traps. They are common throughout Europe and North America.

71 The largest orb webs are built by tropical golden orb-web spiders. Their threads can measure several metres, and the web itself can measure up to 2 metres wide. The webs are so large they can even trap birds that fly into them!

Funnel web spiders

72 Australian funnel webs are amongst the most dangerous spiders in the world. A single bite can cause a person pain, blindness, difficulty in breathing and sometimes death. Strangely, dogs, cats and rabbits are unaffected by their bite.

▶ Sydney funnel web spiders have huge fangs and deadly venom. Males are more venomous than females.

The fangs inject a venom that causes great pain

Dark body with strong, thick legs

73 Funnel web spiders use untidy silken sheets to create tunnels. They hide at one end of the tunnel and wait for their prey to step onto a flat sheet at its opening. *Tegenaria* are a group of funnel web house spiders. They spin tunnels in dark corners, and are very hairy and extremely fast. They live in Europe and North America.

QUIZ

These spider words have been muddled up. Can you rearrange the letters?

ENMOV
EBBCOW
LINGSPERID
LISK

Answers:
VENOM COBWEB SPIDERLING SILK

▶ A ladybird larva struggles to escape from a dense web of silken fibres. The movement alerted this labyrinth spider, which has rushed to attack.

74 Labyrinth spiders build enormous silk webs outside their tunnel lairs. The webs are a mass of threads that drape over and between low bushes. Although the threads are not especially sticky, when an insect flies into them, it falls down onto a silken sheet below. The spider can sense the movement instantly, as the threads twitch, and races to the spot where the insect has fallen.

▼ The woodlouse touches the threads, alerting the tube-web spider in its hole.

75 Tube-web spiders don't catch fish, but they do use fishing lines! The spiders hide inside their tunnels, with slender threads of silk stretching out from the entrance. One or two legs rest on the fishing lines, and when they feel movement, they put out more feet to work out exactly where their prey is. They make a last minute dash, grab their prey, give it a venomous bite and return to the tunnel to eat.

Widows and wolves

76 The black widow spider has a fearsome reputation, but it is usually timid. These American arachnids often lurk in dark corners of houses where people put their fingers or toes. Disturbing a female black widow might make her bite. Her venom causes great pain and sometimes death.

▲ A female black widow has a shiny black body and a red hourglass shape on the underside of her abdomen.

◀ Katipos live in New Zealand, where their name means 'night-stinger'.

77 Black widows belong to a group of arachnids called cobweb or comb-footed spiders. Sticky drops are spread around their messy webs to glue prey in place. Once an insect is trapped, most of the threads around it snap, and the insect springs upwards to be grabbed by the waiting spider.

▲ Australian redbacks belong to the same family as black widows and katipos. They rarely leave their webs, so it is unusual for humans to be bitten.

78 European cobweb spiders build and decorate their homes. They hang silken tubes from their webs, and cover them with bits of plant and soil to disguise them from predators while they rest inside.

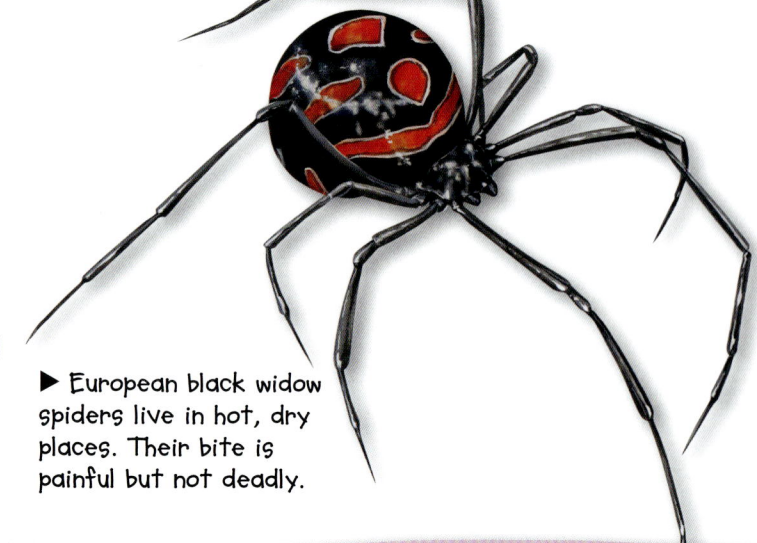

▶ European black widow spiders live in hot, dry places. Their bite is painful but not deadly.

◀ A female black widow has a shiny black body and a red hourglass shape on the underside of her abdomen.

79 Wolf spiders have two large main eyes that help them to see and follow their prey during the day. However, their eyesight is not perfect, and they recognize their prey by the beating of its wings, or the vibrations caused by the way it walks.

▶ Wolf spiders are not as scary as they look. These large, hairy, ground-dwelling hunters prowl around looking for prey, but they are harmless to humans.

80 Male wolf spiders use sign language to tell females they are on the lookout for a mate. They wave their palps around in a special pattern to attract a female's attention and tell her what species they are.

I DON'T BELIEVE IT!
Female Australian redbacks expect males to spend at least 100 minutes 'dancing' before mating can take place. If a male's courtship doesn't impress the female, she eats him!

Jumping spiders

▲ This jumping spider is pouncing on a hoverfly. Jumping spiders appear to be able to plan their attacks — they move around prey or climb to better positions before picking the best time to leap.

81 **The family of jumping spiders is the largest spider family.** There are more than 5000 species, and they are considered to be the most advanced of all spiders. Jumping spiders are active during the day and are often brightly coloured. They are the most athletic of all arachnids!

82 **Jumping spiders are hunters rather than web-builders.** Once they catch sight of their prey and are close enough, they leap, pouncing on the victim and delivering a deadly bite. When jumping spiders leap they always leave a dragline, or safety thread, behind, so if they fall they can climb back up.

83 **These spiders have extraordinary eyesight.** They are able to focus their eyes on an object in front of them and judge its distance away. They can even adjust their retinas — a light sensitive layer inside their eyes — to get a better picture.

QUIZ

If a jumping spider is 10 millimetres long and leaps 20 times its own length, how far will it have travelled? What is that distance in centimetres and in metres?

Answer:
10 x 20 = 200 millimetres
200 millimetres = 20 centimetres or 0.2 metre

84 **Scientists think that jumping spiders may be the brainiest of all arachnids.** They can use information from their eyes to judge speed, angles and distances, as well as determine if a creature is a predator or prey. Most spiders need to use other sensory information, such as vibrations and smell.

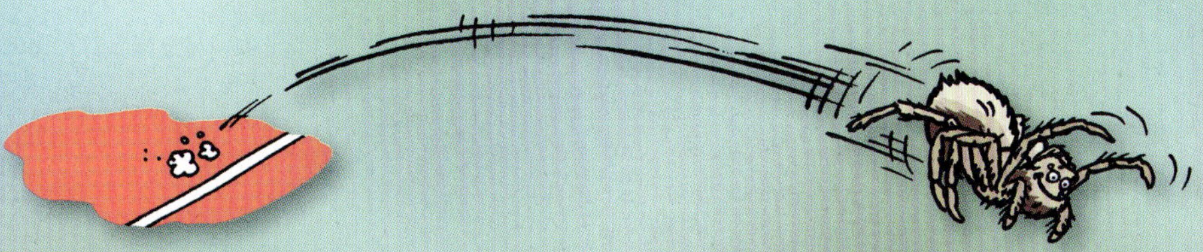

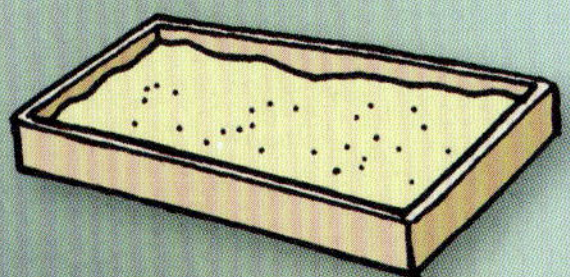

85 **Some jumping spiders can leap more than 20 times their own body length.** Jumping spiders use their third and fourth pairs of legs to leap, but no one knows what other tricks they might use to achieve their record-breaking long-jumps.

▼ A jumping spider's four main eyes focus on its prey, such as this cricket. The four smaller eyes can detect movement.

Tarantulas

86 Tarantulas, or bird-eating spiders, mostly live in warm and wet tropical places. Tarantulas hunt their prey rather than build webs. They usually hunt insects, although larger ones can catch frogs, lizards and even small mammals, such as mice.

87 King baboon spiders hiss at their attackers. They are powerful predators and hunt other spiders, chicks, reptiles and frogs. When attacked, king baboon spiders rear up on their back legs to show off their large chelicerae, and make a loud hissing noise by rubbing their hairy legs together.

▶ Like other tarantulas, a king baboon spider relies on its size as much as its venom to overpower its prey.

▼ Tarantulas build burrows under rocks, hide beneath logs or rest in silk-lined tunnels.

I DON'T BELIEVE IT!
Tarantulas are the heaviest of all spiders. A female goliath bird-eating spider weighed 155 grams — more than a newborn kitten!

88 **Tarantulas don't have good eyesight.** They hunt at night and rely on their touch-sensitive hairs to feel vibrations and movement. A hunting tarantula dashes from its burrow to grab prey, piercing it with large, venomous fangs that are up to 2 centimetres long.

▶ An angry tarantula brushes its abdomen with its legs to fire irritating hairs into the air.

89 **If threatened, a tarantula can flick hairs from its abdomen at an attacker.** The hairs are very irritating to mammals, including humans. Despite this, many people enjoy keeping tarantulas, especially Mexican red-knee tarantulas, as pets.

▼ Hawk wasps prey on tarantulas. Some wasps lay their eggs in a spider's body and others feast on them.

90 **Tarantulas have few natural predators, except certain wasps.** These insects are parasites, which means they live off another animal. The wasp uses her sting to paralyze a spider and lay her eggs inside its body. When the eggs hatch, the larvae feed on the spider's body while it is still alive.

Spiders and us

91 **Many people are scared of spiders.** This fear has led to spiders appearing in stories and myths. An extreme fear of spiders is called arachnophobia. Someone who likes spiders is called an arachnophile. Very few spiders actually pose any threat to humans.

▲ Tarantulas are not ideal pets. They bite, their hairs can be harmful and being handled may cause them stress.

▼ Cooking spiders makes their venom harmless. They are sold as a popular street snack in Cambodia.

92 **European tarantulas gave rise to a wild dance called 'the tarantella'.** These spiders belong to a different family to the bird-eating tarantulas. They were named after the Italian town of Taranto, where it was believed that the effects of a spider bite could only be relieved by performing a frenzied dance – the tarantella.

93 **Some people like eating spiders.** In Cambodia, Southeast Asia, spider catchers use sticks to entice tarantulas from their burrows. They are caught, fried, and served with garlic and salt.

94 **A popular children's book tells the story of a spider called Charlotte.** In the story, the clever spider forms a friendship with Wilbur the pig, and uses her silk-spinning skills to save him when danger looms.

95 **Spider powers were the inspiration for one of the greatest comic book heroes of all time.** In the story of Spider-Man, Peter Parker fights crime with the help of web-shooters, spider sense, great strength, and the ability to climb walls and cling to ceilings.

▲ E B White wrote *Charlotte's Web* more than 50 years ago, but it is still a much-loved tale.

▼ The Spider-Man stories have been turned into successful cartoons and action movies. This is a scene from *Spider-Man 2* (2004).

SOS – save our spiders

96 Spiders are almost everywhere. They are one of the planet's most successful groups of animals. Spiders may be great survivors, but when their habitats are destroyed, their numbers quickly fall. The best way to save our spiders is to protect the habitats where they live.

97 Ladybird spiders are becoming rare because their heathland habitats are being destroyed. These spiders are hard to see because the males only emerge from their burrows at mating time.

▲ Male ladybird spiders have red abdomens that are decorated with black spots. Their black legs have bold white bands on them.

98 One of the world's rarest spiders is the beautiful peacock parachute spider. This tarantula lives in just one forest region of India, where most of the trees have been cut down for firewood and timber.

▲ No one knows how many peacock parachute spiders are still alive because they are so rare and hard to find.

I DON'T BELIEVE IT!
Scientists predict that nearly 30 species of spider could become extinct in the near future.

99 No-eyed big-eyed wolf spiders live in just three volcanic caves on the Hawaiian island of Kaua'i. These arachnids have lost their eyes after living in dark caves for thousands of years or more. There are only about 100 adult no-eyed big-eyed wolf spiders left. They need their habitats to be damp, but pollution and farming have affected them, causing the caves to become too dry.

100 Spiders are an essential part of Earth's web of life. They provide food for many animals and feed on other creatures. Spiders help to maintain the balance of life on our planet, which would be a terrible place without them. A spider in the bath should be admired, not washed away!

▲ A spider scientist (arachnologist) releases a rare spider back into the wild.

▶ A curious house spider eyes a plughole. Once you understand how spiders live, they become fascinating, not frightening, creatures.

Index

Entries in **bold** refer to main subject entries; entries in *italics* refer to illustrations.

A
abdomen 8, *8*, 9
anatomy 8, *8*
ant-mimic spiders *31*
arachnids 8, **12–13**
arachnologists (spider scientists) *47*
arachnophobia 44
Australian redback spiders *38*, 39

B
Bagheera kiplingi spiders 29
ballooning 16
beach wolf spiders *22*
bird dung spiders 11
black widow spiders 38, *38*, 39
body parts 8
Brazilian wandering spiders 33
butterfly larvae 25

C
cave spiders 14, *22*
cephalothorax 8, *8*
Charlotte's Web 45, *45*
chelicerae *8*, 9
claws 17
cobweb spiders 38
cocoons 20, *20*
colours 33
comb-footed spiders 38
cooking spiders 44, *44*
courtship dances 18–19
crab spiders 11, *11*, *14*, 19, *29*, 33, *33*
cucumber spiders 35

D
daddy longlegs spiders 27, *27*
draglines 30, 40

E
eating **28–29**
eggs 20
end-feet 17, *17*
European black widow spiders *38*
European tarantulas 80
extinction 47
eyes 8, 9, 14, *14*, *41*
eyesight 14, 15, 40, 43

F
false scorpions 12
fangs 9, *28*, *36*, *43*
feet (tarsi) 17, *17*
food 21, 28–29
funnel web spiders *30*, 31, **36–37**

G
garden spiders *9*, *18–19*, *34–35*
giant huntsman spiders 10
'glue' 25
gold leaf crab spiders *29*
golden orb-web spiders 35
golden wheel spiders *30*
Goliath bird-eating spiders 10, *10*, 42
green lynx spiders *28*
green tree ants *25*

H
habitats **22–23**, 46
hairs 14, 17, *17*, *32*, *43*, 43
harvestmen 12, 13, *13*
hawk wasps *43*
hibernation 22
house spiders 16, *47*
hunting spiders **32–33**, 40

J K
jumping spiders 14, 18, **40–41**, *40–41*
katipos *38*
king baboon spiders 42, *42*

L M
labyrinth spiders 37, *37*
ladybird spiders 46, *46*
legs 8, 15, 31, *36*
lynx spiders 23, *28*
mating **18–19**, 39
Mexican red-knee tarantulas 14, *43*
midget spiders 11, 35
mites 12, *12*
money spiders 27
moth larvae *25*
moulting 21, *21*
Mount Everest 23
mouse spiders 32
movement **16–17**

N
net-casting spiders *see* ogre-faced spiders
no-eyed big-eyed wolf spiders 47
nocturnal spiders 15
nursery-web spiders 20, *20*

O
ogre-faced spiders *14*, 15
orb-web spiders **34–35**, *34–35*
orbweaver spiders 26, *29*
ornate jumping spiders 19

P R
peacock parachute spiders 46, *46*
peacock spiders 11, *11*
pedipalps 8, 9
pets 44
playing dead 31, *31*
poison *see* venom
predators, avoiding **30–31**
raft spiders 17, *17*
red velvet mites 12

S
Sahara desert 30
scaffold web spiders 18
scopulae 17
scorpion venom 13
scorpions 12, *12*
senses **14–15**
sheet webs 27, *27*
silk 9, 24, **24–25**, 26
silk glands 26
size 10, *10–11*
slit organs 14
smell 14, 15
social spiders *23*
somersaulting spiders 30
spider scientists (arachnologists) *47*
Spider-Man 45, *45*
spiderlings **20–21**, *20–21*
spigots 26, *26*
spinnerets 8, 9, *9*, 26
spiny orb weavers 11
spitting spiders 14, 32, *32*
sun-spiders 13, *13*
Sydney funnel web spiders 36

T
tarantella dance 44
tarantulas 14, 42, **42–43**, *43*, 44, **44**, 46
taste 14, 15
ticks 12, *12*
trapdoor spiders 33, *33*
trapping spiders 34–35
traps 15, 26, 27
tube-web spiders 37, *37*

V W
venom (poison) 9, 13, *28*, 32, *36*, 38
venom (poison) gland *8*, 33
vibration 14
'wandering spiders' **32–33**
wasps 43, *43*
water spiders 22, 23, *23*
weaver ants 25, *25*
web-building 34
webs 15, *20*, 24–25, 26, 27, **34–35**
wolf spiders *6–7*, 16, 19, 21, *21*, **39**, *39*